JESUS

CONTENTS

Palm Sunday 6
    Matthew 21: 1-11; Mark 11: 1-11;
    Luke 19: 28-40; John 11: 55-57; 12: 12-19

Cleansing the Temple 8
    Matthew 21: 12-17; 26: 4; Mark 11: 15-19;
    Luke 19: 45, 46

The Last Supper 10
    Matthew 26: 21-35; Mark 14: 17-31;
    Luke 22: 14-23, 31-34; John 13: 21-38;
    14: 1-31; 18: 1, 2

The Garden of Gethsemane 14
    Matthew 26: 36-56; Mark 14: 32-49;
    Luke 22: 39-52; John 18: 3-12

The Trials of Jesus 18
    Matthew 26: 57-75; 27: 1-26; Luke 22: 54-71;
    23: 1-25; John 18: 12-40

The Crucifixion and Burial 20
    Matthew 27: 27-51, 54-66; Mark 15: 42-47;
    Luke 23: 26-56; John 19: 1-42

The First Easter 24
    Matthew 28: 1-10; Mark 16: 1-8;
    Luke 24: 1-12; John 20: 1-19

The Ascension 28
    Luke 24: 49-51; Acts 1: 3-12

Copyright © 1991 World International Publishing Limited.
Text abridged from The Children's Illustrated Bible.
Published in Great Britain by World International Publishing Limited,
an Egmont Company, Egmont House, P.O. Box 111,
Great Ducie Street, Manchester M60 3BL.

All rights reserved. No part of this publication may be reproduced, stored in a
retrieval system, or transmitted, in any form or by any means, electronic,
mechanical, photocopying, recording or otherwise, without prior permission of
the copyright owners.

Designed by Christine Lawrie
Typeset in Perpetua by Face
Printed in Belgium

British Library Cataloguing in Publication Data

Newman, Marjorie
The Easter story.
1. Christian church. Easter
I. Title II. Lawrie, Robin
263.93
ISBN 0-7498-0120-4

The Easter Story

retold by Marjorie Newman
illustrated by Robin Lawrie

World International Publishing
Manchester

Jesus came to earth to tell people about God's Kingdom of love. But the chief priests and Pharisees would not believe He was God's own son; and they did not understand His message.

Many Jews did believe and began to follow Jesus. The chief priests and Pharisees grew angry and afraid. "He's got to be stopped!" they cried.

And from that day on, they plotted to kill Him.

It was nearly time for the Festival of the Passover. Many people were going to Jerusalem to prepare for it, as was the custom.

Jesus set out with His disciples.

As they came near to Bethphage, He said to two of them, "Go into the village. You'll see a donkey tied up there. She'll have a young colt beside her. I want you to untie the colt, and bring it here to Me."

The disciples nodded. But they were puzzled. Why did Jesus need the donkey?

They went into Bethphage, as Jesus had asked them. Sure enough, there was the colt. They led it away.

Jesus was waiting for them. When the disciples realized He was going to ride on it, they spread their cloaks on the colt's back, to make a saddle.

A crowd had begun to gather. Word spread as quickly as ever.

"Jesus is coming!"

People threw their cloaks down in the road so that Jesus might ride over them. Some people cut branches from the palm trees, and spread them in the road, or waved them like banners.

Now, as Jesus and His disciples moved forward, with Jesus riding on the donkey, there was a crowd in front and behind. People were shouting, "Hosanna! Blessed is He that comes in the name of the Lord! Hosanna to the Son of David! Hosanna in the highest!"

PHARISEE

CHIEF PRIEST

7

So Jesus went to Jerusalem; not sneaking in quietly, afraid of the plots of the chief priests and the Pharisees – but openly, courageously, in the middle of a cheering crowd.

As they entered the city streets, people were asking, "Who is this?"

And Jesus' followers replied proudly, "This is Jesus! Jesus of Nazareth!"

And Jesus went, as the custom was, to the Temple…

In the Temple He stood, anger rising within Him as He saw what was happening.

Young goats and lambs stood trembling in pens. They were waiting to be bought and used as sacrifices.

Money-changers sat with piles of coins in front of them, ready to change money for the people who wanted to pay the Temple tax.

Jesus saw the money-changers were cheating, giving less change than was due.

He had to show that this was wrong. He scattered the coins. He overturned the tables.

He went to free the animals and birds. And He shouted, "It is written in the Scriptures, 'My house shall be called a house of prayer.' But you have made it a den of thieves!"

The disciples stood and watched. Jesus was already in danger of death. Now, far from appeasing the chief priests and the Pharisees, He was making them angrier than ever…

And the Pharisees and chief priests said amongst themselves, "He'll be leading the people to revolt. He must be killed."

It was the first day of the Festival. Jesus and his disciples were ready to eat the Passover meal together.

Jesus began to be very troubled. "One of you will betray me," He said.

Only Judas knew what He meant. Angry at some of Jesus' words and behaviour, he had promised to hand Him over to the chief priests and Pharisees for thirty pieces of silver.

Now John moved very close to Jesus. "Master," he pleaded, "who is it?"

Jesus answered, "It is he to whom I give the bread." And He handed it to Judas…

Judas met Jesus' eyes. "Surely, not me, Master!" he said.

But Jesus knew. "Go, and do what you have to do," He replied.

And Judas got up, and went out into the night.

During the meal Jesus took the bread, and gave thanks to God for it. Then He broke it, and shared it out amongst them, saying, "Take this, and eat it. It is My body, broken for you. Do this in memory of Me."

Next, He took the wine; gave thanks to God, and poured it out for the disciples, saying, "Drink. This is My blood of the New Testament — God's new covenant with man, sealed with My blood. It is shed for you, and for many, so that your sins may be forgiven… I will drink no more of the fruit of the vine until the day I drink it new in the Kingdom of God. My beloved friends, I shall not be with you much longer. So I give you a new commandment. Love one another, as I have loved you."

"Master, where are You going?" they cried. "We will come with You!"

"You cannot come with Me," Jesus answered gently.

"Why not?" Peter demanded. "I would die for You!"

"Peter," said Jesus, "all of you will desert Me, and you will three times deny knowing Me."

"Never!" cried Peter. "I'll never deny knowing You!"

JUDAS

11

"Don't be troubled! You believe in God – believe in Me, also. In My Father's house there are many rooms. If it wasn't so I would have told you. I go to prepare a place for you. Where I am, there you may be, also. And where I am going you know, and the way you know."

Thomas said, "Lord – we don't know where You are going. So how can we know the way?"

Jesus answered, "I am the way, the truth and the life. No one comes to the Father, except by Me. If you have known Me, you have known the Father."

He looked around at their troubled faces. "If you love Me, obey My words. And I will ask the Father to send you another comforter, who will be able to stay with you for ever. Because I live, you shall live also… Peace I leave with you, My peace I give unto you. Let not your heart be troubled, neither let it be afraid."

And when they had spoken some more, they sang a hymn, and went out into the night.

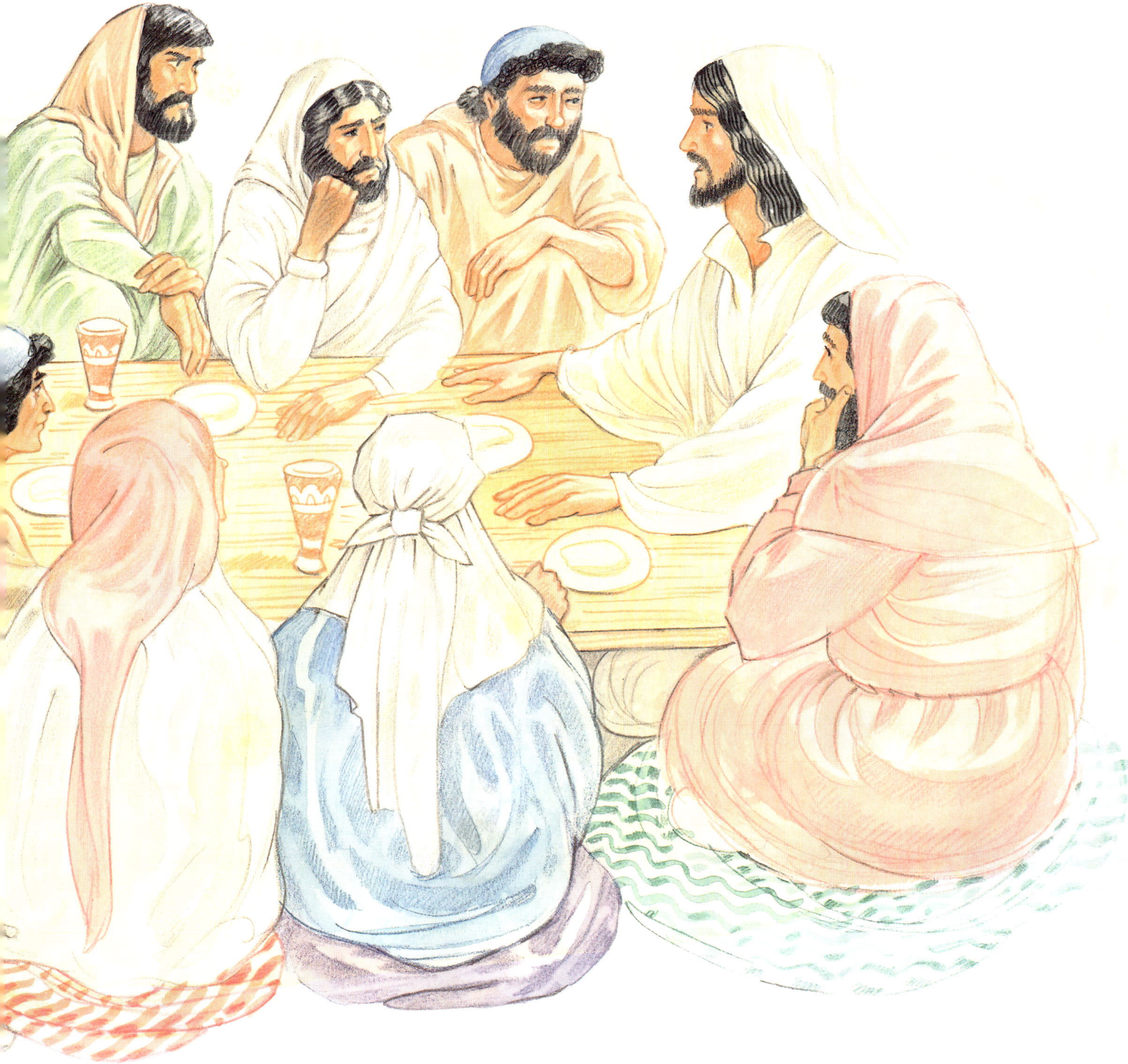

In the Garden of Gethsemane Jesus said to His disciples, "Sit here, while I go and pray. Peter, James, John – come a little further with Me. Keep watch," He said.

He went a little way apart from them, knelt on the ground, and prayed.

Presently He came back to the three. Instead of keeping watch they had fallen asleep.

Jesus said, "Couldn't you watch for just one hour?"

The three disciples woke, ashamed.

"Keep watch," He said a second time.

He went away again to pray. In agony, He said, "Father, if this cup of suffering is the only way – Your will be done…"

He came back to them. Once more they had fallen asleep. Once more He woke them. They could find no words to say to Him.

A third time Jesus prayed. A third time He returned and found them sleeping. He said, "Are you still asleep?" And then, urgently, "Look! The hour has come! Here comes the one who will betray Me!"

The disciples awoke, suddenly aware of the lights of torches and lanterns in the garden – of a crowd carrying sticks and swords – of soldiers of the Temple Guard…

JOHN

15

Jesus stepped forward, calm, quiet; facing the rabble. "Who are you looking for?" He asked.

"Jesus of Nazareth," they answered.

"I am He," Jesus replied.

Judas came pushing his way to the front. And he kissed Jesus, saying, "Master." For this was the secret sign he had arranged with the chief priests.

"Is it with a kiss you betray the Son of Man?" Jesus asked him.

Peter, furious, seized a sword and cut off the ear of the servant of Caiaphas, the high priest.

But Jesus touched the man's ear, and healed him.

"Put down your swords," He said to His followers. "Don't you think I could ask My Father for help? He could send angels to defend Me. But if I do, the Scriptures will not be fulfilled. Do you think I will not obey My Father's will?"

Then He said to the soldiers, "I am Jesus of Nazareth. Let these others go."

And His disciples all deserted Him, and fled.

CAIAPHAS

Now Jesus was in the hands of His enemies. They bound Him, and led Him away to the house of Caiaphas, the high priest. Jesus listened to the many lies which were told about Him; but He remained silent until Caiaphas said, "Tell us. Are You the Son of God?"

There was a hushed pause as everyone waited for the answer. Jesus said, "Yes, as you have said. And you will see the Son of Man sitting at the right hand of God."

"He speaks blasphemy!" cried Caiaphas.

"He must be put to death!" shouted the chief priests and the elders.

And outside the court Peter, in fear, did deny knowing Him.

It was dawn. They took Jesus to Pilate, the Roman governor. Judas saw this. He realized Jesus had been condemned to death and he couldn't bear it. He gave back the silver and went and hanged himself.

Jesus stood silently in front of Pilate.

The chief priests and elders told many more lies, but Jesus answered not one word.

Pilate said, "I can't find anything to charge this man with."

"He has been trying to start a riot in Galilee!" they cried.

"He's from Galilee!" said Pilate, in great relief. "Then it's nothing to do with me. You must take Him to Herod. Herod rules in Galilee."

Herod asked many questions, but Jesus would not say one word. So Herod cruelly made fun of Him and sent Him back to Pilate.

Pilate said, "No one has found this man guilty! I'll have Him whipped, and then let Him go."

"No, no! Free Barabbas instead!" howled the crowd.

Barabbas was a murderer.

"Then what shall I do with Jesus?" asked Pilate.

"Crucify Him!" they yelled.

Pilate was too weak-willed to act against the mob. In front of them all Pilate washed his hands, as a sign that he wasn't making the decision.

So Barabbas was freed, and Jesus was whipped, and handed over to be crucified.

HEROD

BARABBAS

19

The Roman soldiers put a crown of thorns on His head and forced Him to carry a heavy cross to the place called Golgotha.

At the place of execution Jesus' friends watched, helpless, as the soldiers nailed Jesus to the cross with one nail through each hand and foot.

The hammer blows fell, and Jesus was in great pain; but He prayed to God, "Father, forgive them; for they know not what they do."

The cross was lifted and set into place. The soldiers sat down, and began to share out Jesus' clothes between them. They threw a die to see who would win His robe.

As He hung on the cross, many people jeered at Him; and the chief priests and elders said mockingly, "Let Him come down from the cross now, and we will believe Him!" But Jesus would not answer them.

Two thieves were crucified, one on either side of Jesus. One thief was sorry for the wrong he had done. To him,

Jesus said, "Today you will be with Me in paradise."

As Jesus looked down from the cross, He saw His mother, Mary; and His disciple, John, and said, "Woman, behold your son. Son, behold your mother."

Now He was in very great pain. "My God, My God, why hast Thou forsaken Me?" He said.

After a while, He said, "I thirst." So they soaked a sponge in cheap wine, and held it up to His lips.

Soon after that, Jesus said, "It is finished... Father, into Your hands I commit My spirit." And He died.

For the last three hours Jesus was on the cross there was darkness over all the land. As He died, there was a great earthquake, and the curtain which hung in the Temple was ripped in two.

The people were very much afraid. The Roman soldiers who had helped to crucify Him were terrified; and they said, "Surely, this was the Son of God."

GOLGOTHA

To be certain of His death, one of the soldiers pierced Jesus' side with a sword. Blood and water flowed out. The bodies were taken down from the crosses.

The sorrowing disciples wanted to be given Jesus' body, so that they could bury it with loving care. A rich man, Joseph, from Arimathea, went boldly to Pilate, and asked for the body. Pilate gave Joseph permission.

Joseph went to Golgotha with Nicodemus, who had been a secret follower. They took the body, and wrapped it in a new linen sheet, with spices, as was the custom.

Then they placed Jesus' body in the tomb which Joseph had intended for his own use. It was in a garden, close to the place where Jesus had been crucified.

The women who had been with Jesus at the cross also took spices, and went with Joseph. They saw where Jesus' body was buried.

Then Joseph rolled a large stone across the entrance to the tomb, to close it. The sad day was almost over.

It was now the Sabbath day. The chief priests and the Pharisees went to Pilate.

"Sir," they said, "we remember that while this liar was still alive, He said, 'In three days I will be raised from the dead.' Command that a guard be set over the tomb until the third day has passed! Otherwise, His disciples may steal the body, and then spread the rumour that He is alive!"

"Very well," said Pilate. "Go and make the tomb secure."

So the chief priests and the Pharisees put a seal on the stone so that it would be impossible to move it without the seal being broken. And they left well-drilled, highly disciplined Roman soldiers on guard.

And yet…

ROMAN SOLDIER

JOSEPH OF ARIMATHEA

NICODEMUS

23

At sunrise on the Sunday morning Mary Magdalene and some of the other women set out to go to the tomb, taking with them more spices with which to anoint the body of Jesus.

On the way they remembered the huge stone across the entrance. How would they move it? Even as they worried, there was a violent earthquake. In the garden, an angel of the Lord came down, rolled away the stone, and sat on it. When the Roman guards saw him, they fainted in terror.

Before the women reached the tomb, the angel had gone – and the soldiers had fled. Mary Magdalene, who was in front of the others, saw that the stone had been rolled away. She ran back to find Peter and John.

Now the other women arrived at the tomb. Fearfully, they crept inside... Jesus' body was no longer there! And suddenly, two angels stood beside them.

"Don't be afraid!" said the angels. "You are looking for Jesus, who was crucified. But why are you looking for the living among the dead? He is not here! He is risen! Give this message to His disciples, and Peter."

Then the women remembered that Jesus had said He would rise on the third day.

They hurried to tell the disciples. But Mary Magdalene had already reached Peter and John. "They have taken Him away!" she sobbed.

Peter and John ran to the tomb. John saw the cloths in which Jesus' body had been wrapped. Peter saw the wrappings which had bound Jesus' head lying separately. And he believed.

John and Peter looked at each other. Still not fully understanding, the two returned to the house.

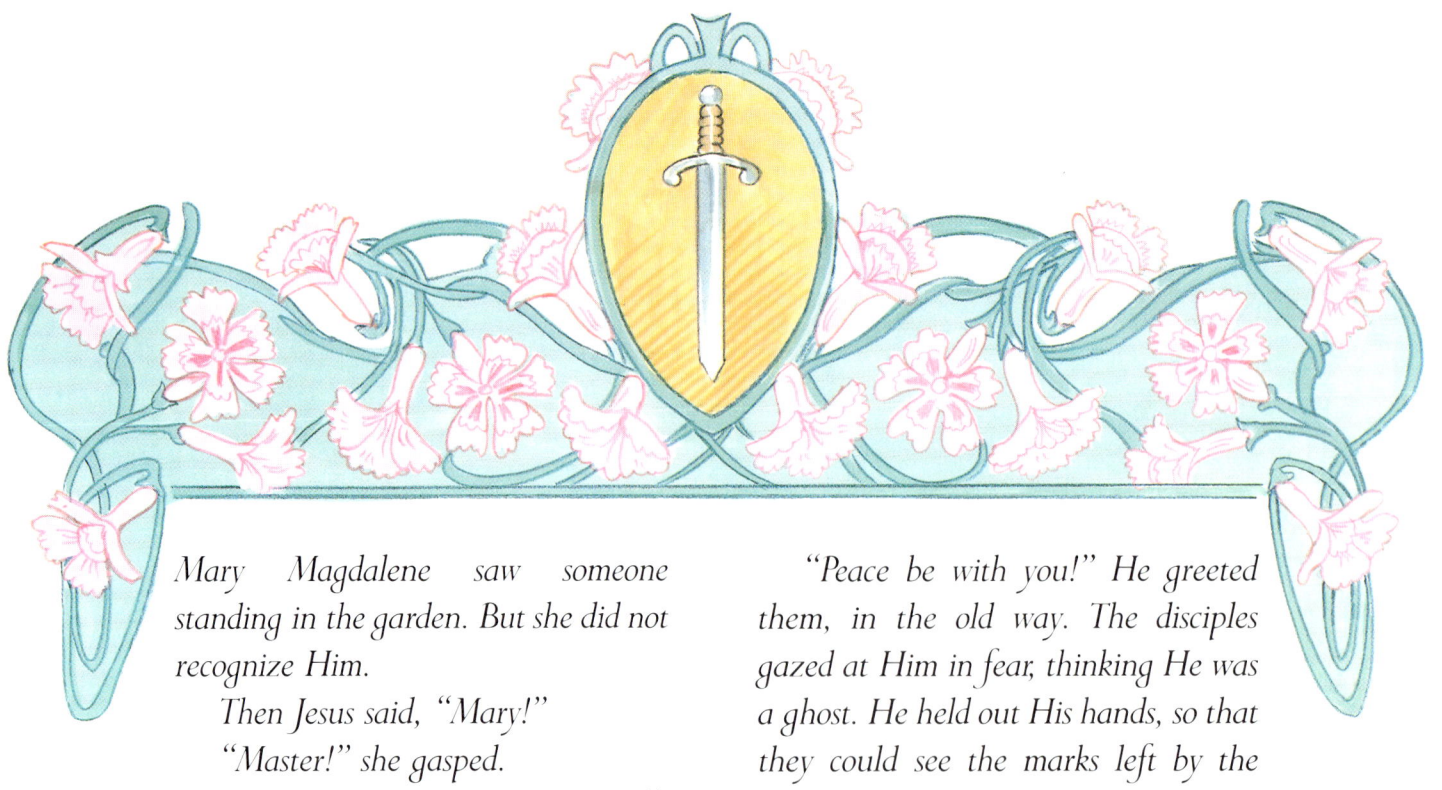

Mary Magdalene saw someone standing in the garden. But she did not recognize Him.

Then Jesus said, "Mary!"

"Master!" she gasped.

"Don't touch Me," Jesus said. "I haven't yet gone back to My Father. But go to My friends, and tell them I am returning to My Father, and your Father. I am returning to God."

Mary hastened back to the disciples, and she gave them His message. But they wouldn't believe He had risen.

Late on the Sunday evening all the disciples except Thomas were gathered in a house, and suddenly, Jesus was standing amongst them.

"Peace be with you!" He greeted them, in the old way. The disciples gazed at Him in fear, thinking He was a ghost. He held out His hands, so that they could see the marks left by the nails. And He showed them His side, where it had been pierced by the Roman soldier's sword. "Touch Me!" He smiled. "You can't touch a ghost!"

Then, seeing they were still unsure, He said, "Have you any food here?"

They gave Him some; and He ate it. At last the disciples could accept the truth. This was no ghost! It was their Master! Risen! Alive! And they were full of joy. Thomas went on doubting until Jesus appeared to him also.

27

For forty days after His crucifixion, Jesus appeared at different times to His disciples. But He knew He could no longer remain on earth with them. He led them out of the city, to the Mount of Olives.

He lifted up His hands to bless them; and even as He did so, He was parted from them; taken up into the skies. And a cloud hid Him, so that they could see Him no longer.

As they gazed upwards, two men dressed in shining white appeared and spoke to them. "Why do you stand gazing upwards into the sky? This Jesus, whom you have seen taken up into Heaven, will one day return in the same way."

Filled with joy, the disciples went back to Jerusalem.

JAMES